Emperor Penguins

by Patricia Trattles

PULL AHEAD BOOKS

Animals

Lerner Publications Company • Minneapolis

To Joan Donaldson, who first brought the Pull Ahead series to my attention and encourged me to submit.

Lerner Publications Company
A division of Lerner Publishing Group
241 First Avenue North
Minneapolis, MN 55401 U.S.A.

Website address: www.lernerbooks.com

Worlds in *italic* type are explained in a glossary on page 30.

Library of Congress Cataloging-in-Publication Data

Trattles, Patricia, 1954–
    Emperor penguins / by Patricia Trattles.
      p.   cm. — (Pull ahead books)
    Includes index.
    ISBN-13: 978-0-8225-3484-6 (lib. bdg. : alk. paper)
    ISBN-10: 0-8225-3484-3 (lib. bdg. : alk. paper)
    1. Emperor penguin—Juvenile literature. I. Title.
    II. Series.
    QL696.S473T73 2006
    598.47—dc22   2005009806

Manufactured in the United States of America
1 2 3 4 5 6 — JR — 11 10 09 08 07 06

What are those dark shapes?

They are emperor penguins marching in a line! They look like they are in a parade.

Waddle, waddle.

Whee! Emperor penguins slide
across the snow on their fat bellies.

Emperor penguins live in Antarctica.
Antarctica is Earth's coldest place.

It is covered with ice all year long.
How do emperor penguins stay warm?

Fat under their skin keeps them warm. And their tiny feathers keep out cold water.

Other kinds
of penguins
live in
Antarctica
too.

But emperors are the biggest penguins. They are about as tall as second graders!

Water surrounds Antarctica. Splash!
The penguins dive into the sea.

Emperor penguins' small wings are not built for flying.

But they are good for swimming.

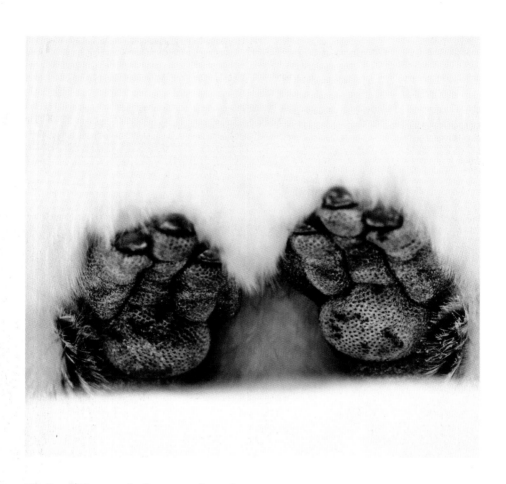

Webbed feet help emperor penguins steer in the water.

Zoom! As emperor penguins swim, they eat fish and *squid*.

Leopard seals eat penguins. Leopard seals are *predators*. Predators hunt and eat other animals.

How do emperor penguins stay safe?

A penguin's feathers help it hide.

Its white belly feathers blend into the cold sky and snow. Its black feathers match the dark water.

In late fall, emperor penguins leave the sea. They go to their *rookery*.

A rookery is where penguins raise their families.

Pairs of emperors do a special dance at the rookery.

After the dance, the mother penguin lays an egg.

The father scoops the egg onto his feet. He covers it with baggy belly skin. This skin is called a *brood pouch*.

The brood pouch keeps the egg warm.

The mother goes back to the sea
to eat.

The father penguins stand on the ice.
They stand very still for nine weeks.

How long can you stand still?

Crack, crack.
An egg
hatches.
Out pops
an emperor
penguin
chick!

The chick is covered in soft
gray feathers called *down*.

The chick sits on its father's feet.
The chick is safe and cozy under its
father's brood pouch.

Finally, the mother returns.
The baby sits on her feet.

Penguin
parents take
turns caring
for their
chick. One
parent keeps
it warm.

The other parent brings food from the sea. The parent uses its beak to feed the chick.

Before long, the chicks get too big
to stand on their parents' feet.

Then they stay together in a group
called a *crèche*.

The chicks grow quickly. Soon they will lose their fluffy down and grow black and white feathers.

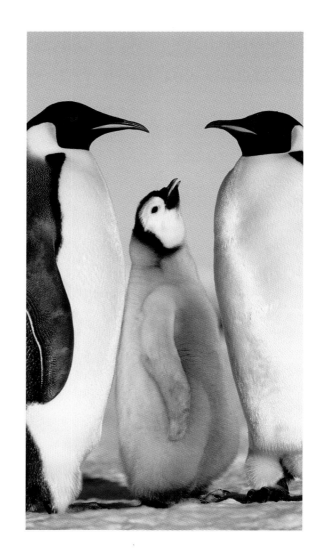

Waddle, waddle. Whee! The young emperor penguins go to the sea.

They are the newest members of the penguin parade.

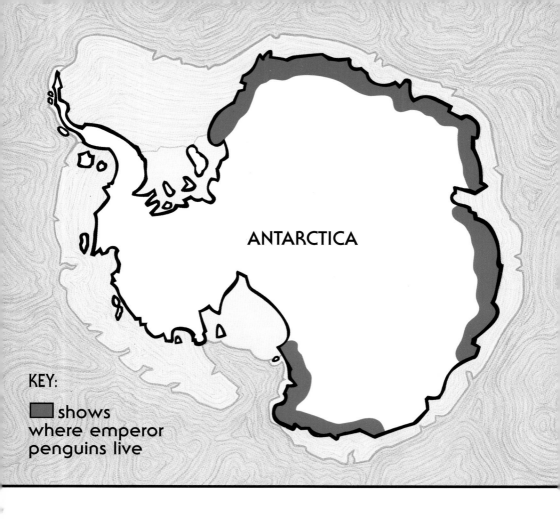

KEY:

█ shows
where emperor
penguins live

ANTARCTICA

🖑 This is a map of Antarctica.
Where do emperor penguins live?

28

Parts of an Emperor Penguin's Body

beak

eye

feathers

wing

tail

brood pouch

leg

webbed foot

29

Glossary

brood pouch: extra skin on a penguin's lower belly. It covers the egg or chick and keeps it safe and warm.

chick: a baby emperor penguin

crèche: a group of older penguin chicks who are too big to stand on their parents' feet. They huddle together for warmth and safety.

down: the soft, fluffy feathers that cover an emperor penguin chick. As chicks grow, their down is replaced with adult feathers.

predators: animals that eat other animals

rookery: a place where emperor penguins lay their eggs and where the chicks hatch

squid: a long, slender sea animal that is similar to an octopus

webbed: having the toes connected by a piece of skin

Further Reading and Websites

Donaldson, Madeline. *Antarctica*. Minneapolis: Lerner Publications Co., 2005.

Hewett, Joan. *A Penguin Chick Grows Up*. Minneapolis: Carolrhoda Books, 2004.

National Geographic Kids. *Creature Feature: Emperor Penguins*.
http://www.nationalgeographic.com/kids/creature_feature/0101/penguins.html

Index

About the Author

Patricia Trattles grew up in Midland, Michigan. After college, she lived in Indiana, Missouri, and Oregon before moving back to Michigan in 2001. She thinks penguins are some of the most adorable and fascinating creatures, and the more she learns about them, the more she loves them. Patricia currently lives in Holland, Michigan, with her husband, Dave, and their two daughters, Erin and Leah. Also residing at the Trattles household is a fat black cat named Ebony. Ebony may not be a penguin, but she sure does waddle like one!

Photo Acknowledgments

The photographs in this book are reproduced through the courtesy of: © Fritz Pölking, front cover, pp. 4, 6, 7, 8, 21, 22, 23, 25, 27, 31; © Royalty-Free/CORBIS, pp. 3, 10; © kevinschafer.com, pp. 5, 16, 17, 24, 26; © Galen Rowell/CORBIS, pp. 9, 11, 15; © Frans Lanting/CORBIS, pp. 12, 20; © Norbert Wu/Minden Pictures, p. 13; © Deneb Karentz, p. 14; © Frans Lanting/Minden Pictures, p. 18; © Marc Chamberlain/SeaPics.com, p. 19.